PRINCEWILL LAGANG

Oracle of Omaha: Decoding Warren Buffett's Investment Wisdom

First published by PRINCEWILL LAGANG 2023

Copyright © 2023 by Princewill Lagang

All rights reserved. No part of this publication may be reproduced, stored or transmitted in any form or by any means, electronic, mechanical, photocopying, recording, scanning, or otherwise without written permission from the publisher. It is illegal to copy this book, post it to a website, or distribute it by any other means without permission.

Princewill Lagang asserts the moral right to be identified as the author of this work.

First edition

This book was professionally typeset on Reedsy. Find out more at reedsy.com

Contents

1	Introduction	1
2	The Genesis of Genius	3
3	The Art of Value Investing	6
4	The Berkshire Hathaway Portfolio	9
5	The Sage's Circle: Buffett's Investment Principles in Action	12
6	Mastering the Market: Buffett's Lessons on Risk and...	15
7	The Philosopher's Stone: Buffett's Ethical and Governance...	18
8	The Next Chapter: Adapting Buffett's Wisdom for Modern...	21
9	The Lasting Legacy: Warren Buffett's Impact on Investing and...	24
10	The Road Ahead: Navigating the Future of Investing	27
11	A Call to Action: Applying Buffett's Wisdom Today	30
12	The Community of Investors: Sharing Buffett's Legacy	33
13	The Evergreen Oracle: Sustaining Buffett's Legacy	36
14	Summary	39

1

Introduction

In the realm of finance and investment, few names carry the weight and wisdom as that of Warren Buffett, the Oracle of Omaha. With a career spanning decades and an unparalleled track record, Buffett has become a beacon of financial success and a source of inspiration for investors worldwide. "Oracle of Omaha: Decoding Warren Buffett's Investment Wisdom" invites you on a captivating journey through the life, principles, and enduring legacy of this legendary figure.

Chapter by chapter, we'll unravel the layers of Buffett's investment philosophy, exploring the key principles that have propelled him to the summit of the financial world. From his early years and formative experiences to the strategic intricacies of his investment decisions, this book serves as a guide for both novice and seasoned investors seeking to understand and apply the timeless wisdom of the Oracle.

As we navigate through Buffett's iconic portfolio, decoding his principles in action, and examining how he adapts to the challenges of the modern financial landscape, readers will gain practical insights into constructing and managing a resilient investment kingdom. We'll explore not only the numerical aspects of investing but also the ethical foundations that have set Buffett apart, making integrity and transparency essential components of his enduring success.

The book extends beyond a mere exploration of Buffett's past triumphs. It provides a roadmap for the future, addressing how his principles can be adapted to navigate emerging trends, technological disruptions, and a growing emphasis on sustainable and responsible investing. Each chapter is a stepping stone, guiding readers towards building their own investment legacy while contributing positively to the global community.

As we embark on this journey through the life and wisdom of Warren Buffett, let us not only seek to understand the mechanics of his success but also to embrace the enduring principles that have made him a true Oracle of the financial world.

2

The Genesis of Genius

Title: Oracle of Omaha: Decoding Warren Buffett's Investment Wisdom

In the heart of the American Midwest, where the plains stretch endlessly and the Missouri River winds its way through the landscape, there lies a city that is synonymous with one of the greatest financial minds of our time. Omaha, Nebraska, may not be a bustling financial hub like Wall Street, but it is the birthplace and headquarters of an investment legend - Warren Buffett.

1.1 The Making of an Oracle

Warren Edward Buffett, born on August 30, 1930, in Omaha, emerged from humble beginnings to become the Oracle of Omaha, a title bestowed upon him for his seemingly supernatural ability to navigate the complexities of the stock market. This chapter delves into the early life of Warren Buffett, exploring the influences and experiences that shaped his investment philosophy.

1.2 A Childhood Fascination

From a young age, Buffett displayed an unusual affinity for numbers and an innate curiosity about the world of business. Raised during the Great Depression, he witnessed the economic hardships of the time, instilling in him a frugality that would become a hallmark of his personal and investment life. As a teenager, he immersed himself in financial books and, at the tender age of eleven, made his first investment in three shares of Cities Service Preferred at $38 per share. Little did the world know that this was just the beginning of an extraordinary journey.

1.3 The Mentorship of Benjamin Graham

The roots of Warren Buffett's investment philosophy can be traced back to his time at Columbia Business School, where he studied under the renowned economist and investor, Benjamin Graham. Graham's seminal work, "Security Analysis," and "The Intelligent Investor," left an indelible mark on Buffett's approach to investing. This chapter explores the profound impact Graham had on shaping Buffett's understanding of value investing, emphasizing the importance of intrinsic value and a margin of safety.

1.4 The Birth of Berkshire Hathaway

As Buffett's knowledge and experience grew, so did his ambitions. The story of Berkshire Hathaway, initially a textile manufacturing company, unfolds as Buffett transforms it into a diversified conglomerate and an investment vehicle that would generate staggering returns over the years. This chapter provides insights into the pivotal moments that led to the birth of Berkshire Hathaway and its evolution into the behemoth it is today.

1.5 Lessons from the Stock Market Battlefield

Warren Buffett's journey as an investor has been a series of triumphs and challenges. This section delves into some of the early setbacks and lessons learned by Buffett, exploring how these experiences contributed to the refinement of his investment strategy. From the textile industry woes to the tumultuous market conditions of the 1970s, each obstacle became a stepping stone in Buffett's quest for investment mastery.

1.6 The Essence of Buffett's Investment Philosophy

As we conclude this chapter, we distill the fundamental principles that underpin Warren Buffett's investment philosophy. From the concept of economic moats to the emphasis on long-term thinking, these principles serve as the guiding light for investors seeking to decode the Oracle of Omaha's success. Through anecdotes, quotes, and historical context, readers gain a deeper understanding of the core tenets that continue to shape Buffett's investment decisions.

Join us on this journey into the heartland of America, where a quiet yet brilliant mind has left an indelible mark on the world of finance. The Oracle of Omaha awaits, and the wisdom he imparts promises to unravel the secrets behind his extraordinary success.

3

The Art of Value Investing

Title: "Intrinsic Value Unveiled"

2.1 The Essence of Value Investing

Warren Buffett's investment philosophy is synonymous with the concept of value investing. In this chapter, we delve deep into the core principles that define this approach. From understanding the intrinsic value of a company to the concept of a margin of safety, we unravel the layers of Buffett's methodical and disciplined strategy. Value investing, as practiced by the Oracle of Omaha, is not just a set of rules but a mindset—a way of thinking that prioritizes long-term value over short-term market fluctuations.

2.2 Intrinsic Value: The North Star

At the heart of Buffett's investment philosophy lies the concept of intrinsic value—the true worth of a business. This section explores how Buffett calculates intrinsic value and why he considers it the most critical factor in investment decision-making. From assessing a company's financial statements to projecting future cash flows, understanding intrinsic value is the key to unlocking the potential for sustained returns.

2.3 Economic Moats: Building Fortresses of Investment

Buffett often speaks of economic moats—competitive advantages that allow a company to fend off competition and sustain profitability. This chapter examines the various types of economic moats, including brand strength, cost advantages, network effects, and regulatory advantages. By identifying companies with wide and enduring moats, investors can align their portfolios with the Oracle's strategy for long-term success.

2.4 The Margin of Safety: A Shield in Turbulent Times

In the unpredictable world of finance, Buffett emphasizes the importance of a margin of safety—an extra cushion that protects investors from unforeseen risks. This section explores how the margin of safety acts as a shield against market volatility and unexpected downturns. By buying stocks at prices below their intrinsic value, investors can position themselves to weather storms and capitalize on opportunities that may arise.

2.5 The Psychology of Market Mr. Market

Warren Buffett often likens the stock market to Mr. Market, an unpredictable character whose mood swings create opportunities for astute investors. This chapter explores the psychological aspects of investing, delving into Buffett's advice to be fearful when others are greedy and greedy when others are fearful. Understanding the emotional currents of the market is crucial for investors looking to navigate the waves of uncertainty and capitalize on mispriced opportunities.

2.6 Patience and Perseverance: The Buffett Way

Buffett's investment success is not built on quick gains or market timing;

instead, it is rooted in patience and perseverance. This section examines how Buffett's long-term perspective sets him apart in an era dominated by short-term thinking. By holding quality investments for extended periods, Buffett has demonstrated the power of time in compounding wealth and the importance of staying the course in the face of market fluctuations.

As we unravel the layers of value investing, readers will gain a comprehensive understanding of how Warren Buffett's keen insights and disciplined approach have made him a maestro in the art of identifying undervalued assets and building wealth over time. The principles explored in this chapter serve as a blueprint for investors seeking to adopt the Oracle of Omaha's time-tested strategies.

4

The Berkshire Hathaway Portfolio

Title: "Building a Castle of Wealth: Inside Buffett's Investment Kingdom"

3.1 The Evolution of Berkshire Hathaway's Portfolio

Berkshire Hathaway, under Warren Buffett's stewardship, has become a conglomerate unlike any other. This chapter delves into the evolution of the company's portfolio, tracing its journey from a textile manufacturing business to a diversified powerhouse of investments. Through mergers, acquisitions, and strategic moves, Buffett has transformed Berkshire Hathaway into a kingdom of wealth, and this section explores the key milestones in this remarkable journey.

3.2 Iconic Holdings: Coca-Cola and the Power of Brand

One of the hallmarks of Buffett's investment strategy is his penchant for iconic brands with enduring consumer appeal. Coca-Cola, a flagship holding in the Berkshire Hathaway portfolio, serves as a case study in the power of brand loyalty and the stability it brings to an investment. This chapter examines why Buffett considers such companies as cornerstones of his portfolio and the role they play in providing steady returns over time.

3.3 The Oracle's Banking Empire

Warren Buffett's affinity for the banking sector is a well-known facet of his investment strategy. This section explores the rationale behind his significant investments in banks, including Wells Fargo, Bank of America, and others. From understanding the role of banks in the broader economy to evaluating their financial health, readers gain insights into why Buffett considers well-managed financial institutions as pillars of his investment kingdom.

3.4 Technological Reservations: Buffett's Approach to Tech Stocks

While Berkshire Hathaway's portfolio is diverse, it notably lacked significant investments in technology companies for many years. This chapter examines Buffett's reservations about the tech sector and how, in recent times, he has adapted his strategy by adding tech giants like Apple to the portfolio. The evolution of Berkshire's stance on technology stocks provides valuable lessons in flexibility and adaptability in the ever-changing landscape of the stock market.

3.5 The Insurance Advantage: Float and Underwriting Profits

Berkshire Hathaway's ownership of insurance companies plays a pivotal role in its success. This section explores the concept of "float"—the funds generated from insurance premiums before claims are paid out—and how Buffett has leveraged this unique advantage to finance investments. The chapter also delves into the importance of underwriting discipline in the insurance business and its impact on Berkshire's overall financial health.

3.6 The Oracle's Crystal Ball: Economic Insights and Macro Perspectives

Beyond individual stock picks, Buffett's annual letters and public statements are laden with economic insights and macro perspectives. This chapter explores how Buffett interprets economic indicators, his views on inflation, and the role of interest rates in shaping investment decisions. Understanding the Oracle's macroeconomic lens provides readers with a deeper appreciation of the holistic approach he takes when steering the Berkshire Hathaway ship.

As we navigate through the diverse holdings of Berkshire Hathaway, readers will gain a comprehensive understanding of how Warren Buffett strategically constructs and manages his investment kingdom. From iconic brands to the nuances of the insurance industry, each element of the portfolio reflects the Oracle's wisdom in creating lasting wealth.

5

The Sage's Circle: Buffett's Investment Principles in Action

Title: "Wisdom in Action: Applying Buffett's Tenets to Your Portfolio"

4.1 Circle of Competence: Knowing What You Know

Warren Buffett often speaks about staying within one's circle of competence—the areas where an investor has expertise and a deep understanding. This chapter explores the concept of the circle of competence and how investors can identify and leverage their unique strengths. By staying true to their areas of expertise, readers learn how to make informed investment decisions and avoid the pitfalls of venturing into unfamiliar territories.

4.2 Quality over Quantity: Concentrated Investing

Buffett is known for his concentrated investment approach, favoring a focused portfolio of high-conviction holdings. This section examines the benefits and challenges of concentrated investing, emphasizing the importance of quality over quantity. Through case studies of Berkshire Hathaway's concentrated positions, readers gain insights into how to build a robust portfolio that stands the test of time.

4.3 Embracing Market Volatility: The Contrarian's Advantage

While many investors fear market volatility, Buffett sees it as an opportunity. This chapter explores the Oracle's contrarian mindset and how he views market downturns as a chance to acquire quality assets at discounted prices. By understanding the psychology of fear and greed in the market, readers can learn to embrace volatility and use it to their advantage, just as Buffett has throughout his career.

4.4 Long-Term Vision: The Power of Patience

Buffett's success is built on a foundation of long-term vision and patience. This section explores the benefits of adopting a patient approach to investing, allowing time and compounding to work in favor of the investor. Through historical examples and Buffett's own experiences, readers gain a deeper appreciation for the power of time in wealth creation and the importance of resisting the allure of short-term gains.

4.5 The Art of Stock Selection: Qualitative and Quantitative Factors

Buffett's stock selection process combines qualitative and quantitative analysis. This chapter dissects the Oracle's method of evaluating companies, from understanding their business models and competitive advantages to analyzing financial statements and ratios. By blending the art and science of stock selection, readers can learn to identify investment opportunities that align with Buffett's time-tested criteria.

4.6 The Exit Strategy: Knowing When to Hold and When to Fold

Warren Buffett famously said, "Our favorite holding period is forever." However, there are instances where he exits investments. This section explores the Oracle's exit strategy, examining the factors that may prompt him to sell a stock. By understanding the principles behind selling decisions, readers can navigate their own portfolios with a strategic approach to managing gains and minimizing losses.

As we explore the Sage's Circle, readers will gain practical insights into applying Buffett's investment principles to their own portfolios. From staying within one's circle of competence to embracing market volatility, each chapter provides actionable strategies that align with the Oracle's time-tested wisdom.

6

Mastering the Market: Buffett's Lessons on Risk and Resilience

Title: "Navigating Storms: Risk Management and Resilience in Buffett's World"

5.1 The Oracle's Gambit: Understanding and Managing Risk

In the unpredictable world of finance, risk is an ever-present companion. This chapter explores how Warren Buffett assesses and manages risk in his investment decisions. From the importance of understanding a company's competitive position to evaluating management quality, readers gain insights into the Oracle's risk mitigation strategies. Understanding the art of balancing risk and reward is a crucial aspect of Buffett's approach to wealth creation.

5.2 Market Fluctuations: Buffett's Stoic Approach

Market fluctuations are an inherent part of investing, and Warren Buffett's stoic approach to market ups and downs is a key pillar of his success. This section explores the Oracle's mindset during turbulent times, examining how he maintains a long-term perspective amid short-term market noise. By learning to navigate market emotions and maintain composure, investors can better position themselves for success in the face of uncertainty.

5.3 The Tale of Black Swan Events: Preparing for the Unpredictable

While some events are unforeseeable, Buffett's approach to risk involves preparing for the unexpected. This chapter delves into how the Oracle of Omaha positions his portfolio to withstand black swan events—unexpected and severe market disruptions. By building resilience into investment strategies and maintaining a margin of safety, readers can learn to fortify their portfolios against unforeseen challenges.

5.4 The Buffett Put: Optionality in Investments

Buffett is known for his emphasis on optionality—the ability to seize opportunities that may arise in the future. This section explores how the Oracle structures his investments to retain flexibility and capitalize on changing market conditions. By incorporating optionality into their own investment strategies, readers can learn to adapt to evolving circumstances and position themselves for success in dynamic markets.

5.5 The Berkshire Hathaway Annual Meeting: A Lesson in Transparency

The annual shareholder meeting of Berkshire Hathaway has become a legendary event in the investment world. This chapter explores how Buffett uses this platform to communicate openly with shareholders, providing insights into the company's performance, strategy, and the economic landscape. The transparency displayed at these meetings offers readers a lesson in effective communication and the importance of aligning with companies that prioritize shareholder interests.

5.6 The Buffett Indicator: Gauging Market Valuations

Buffett's views on market valuations are encapsulated in what is often referred to as the "Buffett Indicator," which compares the total market capitalization of all publicly traded stocks to the gross domestic product (GDP). This chapter examines the significance of the Buffett Indicator and how investors can use it as a tool to gauge overall market conditions. By understanding market valuations, readers can make more informed decisions about portfolio allocation and risk management.

In this chapter, readers will gain a comprehensive understanding of how Warren Buffett approaches risk and resilience in the dynamic world of investing. From managing market fluctuations to preparing for black swan events, each lesson provides valuable insights into the Oracle's strategies for navigating the uncertainties of the financial landscape.

7

The Philosopher's Stone: Buffett's Ethical and Governance Foundations

Title: "Integrity, Ethics, and Governance: The Bedrock of Buffett's Kingdom"

6.1 The Buffett Code: Ethics in Action

Warren Buffett is not only celebrated for his investment acumen but also for his unwavering commitment to ethical business practices. This chapter delves into the Buffett Code—an unwritten set of ethical principles that guide his decisions. From transparency and honesty in financial reporting to fair treatment of shareholders, readers gain insights into how ethical considerations form the foundation of Buffett's investment kingdom.

6.2 The Shareholder Letter: A Manifesto of Accountability

Warren Buffett's annual letters to Berkshire Hathaway shareholders are more than just financial updates; they are a manifesto of accountability and transparency. This section explores how these letters provide a window into the Oracle's mind, offering candid insights into the company's performance, challenges, and future prospects. By understanding the importance of transparent communication, readers can appreciate the role of accountability in the long-term success of any enterprise.

6.3 Corporate Governance: Buffett's Blueprint for Boardroom Excellence

Effective corporate governance is a cornerstone of Buffett's investment strategy. This chapter examines how he evaluates a company's governance structure, emphasizing the importance of independent and capable directors. By understanding the Oracle's criteria for assessing governance, readers can make informed decisions about the companies they choose to invest in and the standards they expect from corporate leadership.

6.4 The Buffett Test: Investing in Management

While financial metrics are crucial, Buffett places equal importance on the quality of a company's management. This section explores the Buffett Test—a qualitative assessment of a company's leadership. By evaluating factors such as integrity, vision, and capital allocation skills, readers can learn to identify companies led by exceptional management teams, a key component of Buffett's investment checklist.

6.5 Philanthropy and Social Responsibility: Buffett's Pledge

Warren Buffett, along with Bill and Melinda Gates, initiated the Giving Pledge—a commitment by billionaires to give away the majority of their wealth to address society's most pressing problems. This chapter explores Buffett's philanthropic philosophy and the role of social responsibility in his worldview. By understanding the importance of giving back, readers can appreciate how ethical business practices extend beyond the boardroom to contribute to the greater good.

6.6 The Oracle's Legacy: Teaching Beyond the Numbers

Warren Buffett's legacy extends beyond his financial success; it encompasses the lessons he imparts to the next generation of investors. This section explores Buffett's commitment to education and mentorship, examining how he shares his wisdom through books, lectures, and the annual Berkshire Hathaway shareholder meetings. By understanding the importance of continuous learning and mentorship, readers can embark on their own journey to master the art of investing.

In this chapter, readers will explore the ethical and governance foundations that underpin Warren Buffett's investment kingdom. From the Buffett Code to the philanthropic endeavors that define his legacy, each section provides valuable insights into the ethical considerations that contribute to the sustained success of both Berkshire Hathaway and the Oracle of Omaha himself.

8

The Next Chapter: Adapting Buffett's Wisdom for Modern Markets

Title: "Buffett in the Digital Age: Navigating Contemporary Challenges"

7.1 Technological Disruption: A New Landscape for Investors

The digital age has brought unprecedented changes to the business landscape. This chapter explores how Warren Buffett's timeless principles adapt to the challenges and opportunities presented by technological disruption. From the rise of innovative industries to the impact of artificial intelligence, readers gain insights into how Buffett's wisdom remains relevant in navigating the complexities of the modern market.

7.2 Fintech and Cryptocurrencies: Buffett's Stance on Innovation

The emergence of fintech and cryptocurrencies has challenged traditional notions of finance. This section examines Buffett's stance on these innovations, exploring how he evaluates their potential impact on the investment landscape. By understanding the Oracle's approach to emerging technologies, readers can assess the risks and rewards of incorporating these assets into their portfolios.

7.3 Environmental, Social, and Governance (ESG) Investing: A Paradigm Shift

In recent years, there has been a growing emphasis on ESG investing—considering environmental, social, and governance factors in investment decisions. This chapter explores how Buffett's principles align with the evolving focus on sustainable and socially responsible investing. By incorporating ESG considerations, readers can learn to build portfolios that align with both financial goals and broader societal values.

7.4 Globalization and Geopolitical Risks: Navigating an Interconnected World

The interconnectedness of global markets introduces new challenges, from geopolitical risks to trade tensions. This section examines how Buffett navigates the complexities of international investing and manages risks in a world where economic events in one corner of the globe can reverberate across markets. By understanding the Oracle's global perspective, readers can adapt their own strategies to the realities of a highly interconnected world.

7.5 The Rise of Index Funds: Buffett's Endorsement and Caution

Index funds have become increasingly popular as a low-cost investment option. This chapter explores Buffett's views on index funds, examining both his endorsement of their simplicity and cost-effectiveness and his caution regarding their blind reliance on market averages. By understanding the nuances of index investing, readers can make informed decisions about incorporating these funds into their portfolios.

7.6 The Legacy of Buffett's Wisdom: Lessons for Future Generations

As we look ahead, this section reflects on the enduring legacy of Warren Buffett's wisdom. It explores how investors can apply the timeless principles learned from the Oracle of Omaha to navigate the ever-changing landscape of the financial markets. By embracing the essence of Buffett's philosophy while adapting to contemporary challenges, readers can embark on their own journey toward financial success.

In this final chapter, readers will explore how Warren Buffett's investment wisdom continues to be a guiding light in the face of contemporary challenges. From technological disruption to the rise of sustainable investing, each section provides insights into how investors can apply Buffett's principles to thrive in the dynamic and evolving landscape of the digital age.

9

The Lasting Legacy: Warren Buffett's Impact on Investing and Beyond

Title: "Beyond Berkshire: Buffett's Enduring Influence"

8.1 The Buffett Effect: Shaping the Investment Landscape

Warren Buffett's impact on the world of investing extends far beyond the walls of Berkshire Hathaway. This chapter explores the Buffett Effect—the profound influence he has had on investment philosophy, strategy, and the very culture of the financial industry. From value investing disciples to the widespread adoption of his principles, readers gain insights into how Buffett has shaped the way investors approach the market.

8.2 The Cult of Personality: Buffett's Enduring Popularity

Warren Buffett's unique combination of financial acumen, humility, and wit has cultivated a cult of personality that transcends the financial world. This section delves into the reasons behind Buffett's enduring popularity, examining how his personal qualities and approachability have made him a revered figure not only in finance but in popular culture. By understanding the Buffett persona, readers can appreciate the human side of the Oracle of Omaha.

8.3 Buffett's Endorsements: Shaping Corporate Behavior

Through his investments and public statements, Buffett has become a de facto advocate for certain business practices and ethical standards. This chapter explores how his influence has shaped corporate behavior, from encouraging transparency to promoting long-term value creation. By understanding the impact of Buffett's endorsements, readers can appreciate the role of shareholder activism and ethical leadership in the corporate world.

8.4 The Giving Pledge: A Philanthropic Legacy

Warren Buffett's commitment to philanthropy is not only a personal choice but a call to action for the world's wealthiest individuals. This section explores the impact of the Giving Pledge, the initiative he co-founded with Bill and Melinda Gates. By examining the philanthropic endeavors inspired by Buffett's pledge, readers gain insights into the broader implications of aligning wealth with social responsibility.

8.5 Lessons Beyond Investing: Wisdom for Life

Beyond the realm of finance, Warren Buffett's life principles and aphorisms offer valuable lessons for navigating the complexities of life. This chapter explores the broader applications of Buffett's wisdom, from personal relationships to decision-making and happiness. By incorporating these life lessons, readers can glean insights into living a fulfilling and principled life.

8.6 The Enduring Oracle: Reflections on a Storied Career

As we conclude this exploration of Warren Buffett's impact, we reflect on the enduring legacy of the Oracle of Omaha. This section provides a retrospective on Buffett's storied career, examining the key milestones, lessons, and contributions that have solidified his place as one of the greatest investors of all time. By understanding the trajectory of Buffett's journey, readers can draw inspiration for their own paths toward financial success and personal fulfillment.

In this final chapter, readers will gain a comprehensive understanding of Warren Buffett's lasting impact on investing, corporate governance, philanthropy, and life beyond finance. As we reflect on the enduring legacy of the Oracle of Omaha, readers are invited to carry forward the lessons learned and apply them to their own endeavors, both in the world of finance and in the broader scope of life.

10

The Road Ahead: Navigating the Future of Investing

Title: "Investing in the Unknown: Adapting Buffett's Legacy to Tomorrow's Challenges"

9.1 The Unpredictable Future: Embracing Uncertainty

As we look to the future, the world of finance is certain to present new challenges and opportunities. This chapter explores the unpredictable nature of the financial landscape and the importance of embracing uncertainty. Drawing from Buffett's own resilience in the face of market fluctuations, readers gain insights into how to navigate the unknown and build robust investment strategies that withstand the tests of time.

9.2 Technological Advancements: Embracing Innovation

The pace of technological advancements shows no signs of slowing down. This section examines how investors can adapt Buffett's principles to the era of artificial intelligence, blockchain, and other emerging technologies. By understanding the role of innovation in shaping the investment landscape, readers can position themselves to capitalize on transformative trends while staying true to the fundamental principles espoused by the Oracle of Omaha.

9.3 Globalization and Economic Shifts: A Changing World Order

The geopolitical and economic landscape is subject to continuous shifts. This chapter explores how investors can navigate the challenges and opportunities presented by globalization, trade dynamics, and geopolitical uncertainties. By drawing parallels to Buffett's approach to international investing, readers gain insights into adapting their portfolios to thrive in a world where borders are increasingly fluid and interconnected.

9.4 Sustainable Investing: A Growing Imperative

The rise of environmental, social, and governance (ESG) considerations is reshaping the investment landscape. This section explores how Buffett's principles align with the growing emphasis on sustainability and responsible investing. By understanding the importance of ESG factors, readers can incorporate these considerations into their investment decisions and contribute to a more sustainable and ethical financial future.

9.5 Generational Shifts: Investing for the Next Era

As demographics and societal norms evolve, the investing landscape is influenced by generational shifts. This chapter examines how the preferences and priorities of different generations, such as Millennials and Gen Z, impact investment trends. By understanding the changing dynamics of investor behavior, readers can adapt their strategies to align with the values and preferences of the next era of market participants.

9.6 The Enduring Principles: Timeless Wisdom for Tomorrow

While the future may be uncertain, certain principles endure. This section distills the timeless wisdom embedded in Buffett's approach to investing, governance, and life. By reflecting on the enduring principles that have guided the Oracle of Omaha, readers can draw inspiration and guidance for their own journeys through the ever-evolving landscape of the financial world.

As we embark on the road ahead, this chapter serves as a guide to adapting Warren Buffett's legacy to the challenges and opportunities of tomorrow. By embracing uncertainty, leveraging technological advancements, and aligning with evolving societal values, readers can navigate the future of investing with a strategic mindset and a commitment to enduring principles.

11

A Call to Action: Applying Buffett's Wisdom Today

Title: "Building Your Investment Kingdom: A Practical Guide to Success"

10.1 The Power of Knowledge: Continual Learning in Investing

Warren Buffett's success is rooted in a deep commitment to knowledge and learning. This chapter emphasizes the importance of continual learning in the world of investing. By exploring diverse sources of information, understanding financial statements, and staying informed about market trends, readers can empower themselves with the knowledge needed to make informed investment decisions.

10.2 Defining Your Circle of Competence: Know What You Know

Buffett's principle of staying within one's circle of competence is a cornerstone of successful investing. This section guides readers in identifying their areas of expertise and aligning their investments accordingly. By recognizing strengths and limitations, investors can build a focused and resilient portfolio that reflects their unique understanding of the market.

10.3 Patience and Discipline: The Art of Long-Term Investing

The enduring success of Warren Buffett is a testament to the power of patience and discipline in investing. This chapter explores the art of long-term investing, emphasizing the benefits of holding quality investments over time and resisting the urge to succumb to short-term market fluctuations. By cultivating patience and discipline, readers can emulate Buffett's approach to building lasting wealth.

10.4 Selecting Quality Investments: Lessons from Buffett's Playbook

Buffett's investment philosophy revolves around selecting quality companies with enduring competitive advantages. This section provides practical guidance on evaluating stocks, understanding financial metrics, and identifying businesses with strong economic moats. By adopting a systematic approach to stock selection, readers can align their portfolios with Buffett's time-tested principles.

10.5 Risk Management: Navigating the Ups and Downs

Understanding and managing risk is a critical aspect of successful investing. This chapter explores practical strategies for assessing and mitigating risk in investment decisions. By incorporating principles such as the margin of safety and diversification, readers can build resilient portfolios that can weather market volatility and uncertainties.

10.6 Incorporating Ethical Considerations: Investing with Integrity

Ethical considerations form the bedrock of Warren Buffett's investment philosophy. This section guides readers in incorporating ethical principles into their investment decisions. By evaluating a company's governance, transparency, and overall ethical stance, investors can align their portfolios with businesses that share their values.

10.7 Giving Back: Philanthropy and Social Responsibility

Warren Buffett's commitment to philanthropy serves as a model for responsible wealth management. This chapter encourages readers to consider the impact of their wealth on society and explore ways to give back. By incorporating philanthropic goals into their financial plans, investors can contribute to positive change while building a legacy beyond financial success.

10.8 Crafting Your Legacy: Lessons Beyond Investing

Beyond the numbers and financial success, this section encourages readers to consider the broader aspects of legacy-building. By reflecting on life lessons, personal values, and the impact they wish to have on the world, investors can craft a legacy that extends beyond their financial portfolios.

As we conclude this journey through the wisdom of Warren Buffett, Chapter 10 serves as a call to action. Readers are encouraged to apply the practical insights gained from Buffett's principles to their own investment strategies. By building a resilient and principled approach to wealth management, readers can embark on a path toward financial success and contribute positively to the world around them.

12

The Community of Investors: Sharing Buffett's Legacy

Title: "Building a Community of Wisdom and Wealth"

11.1 The Wisdom of Collective Knowledge: Learning from Each Other

Warren Buffett's legacy extends beyond individual success to the creation of a community of investors who share insights and experiences. This chapter emphasizes the value of collective knowledge, encouraging readers to engage with and learn from one another. By fostering a community that shares wisdom, investors can enhance their understanding of the market and collectively navigate the complexities of investing.

11.2 Investment Clubs and Networks: Strength in Numbers

Investment clubs and networks provide avenues for like-minded individuals to come together, discuss investment strategies, and pool resources. This section explores the benefits of joining or forming investment clubs, where members can leverage each other's expertise, share research, and collectively make more informed investment decisions. By participating in such communities, investors can tap into the collective wisdom that strengthens individual portfolios.

11.3 Online Forums and Social Media: Digital Spaces for Collaboration

In the digital age, online forums and social media platforms offer spaces for investors to connect, share ideas, and discuss market trends. This chapter explores the opportunities and challenges of engaging in digital investment communities. By leveraging the power of technology, investors can access a wealth of information, diverse perspectives, and real-time discussions that contribute to their growth and knowledge.

11.4 Mentorship and Knowledge Transfer: Guiding the Next Generation

Warren Buffett benefited from the mentorship of Benjamin Graham, and this chapter emphasizes the importance of mentorship in the investing community. By fostering relationships with experienced investors, readers can gain valuable insights, receive guidance, and accelerate their learning curve. Mentorship serves as a bridge for knowledge transfer, connecting seasoned investors with the next generation of wealth builders.

11.5 Investment Education: Empowering the Future

Education is a key pillar of Warren Buffett's philosophy, and this section explores the role of investment education in building a community of informed investors. By supporting and participating in educational initiatives, investors can contribute to the empowerment of future generations. Whether through financial literacy programs or investment-focused curricula, education becomes a catalyst for positive change within the broader community.

11.6 Philanthropy as a Community Endeavor: Amplifying Impact

Inspired by Buffett's commitment to philanthropy, this chapter highlights the potential for collective philanthropic efforts within the investment community. By joining forces to address societal challenges, investors can amplify their impact and contribute to positive change. Through collaborative philanthropy, the community of investors can leave a lasting legacy that extends beyond financial success.

11.7 Strengthening Bonds: Conferences, Summits, and Gatherings

Conferences, summits, and gatherings provide opportunities for investors to come together, network, and share insights. This section explores the benefits of participating in such events, where individuals can engage with thought leaders, attend seminars, and build connections. By strengthening bonds within the investment community, readers can create a supportive network that enhances their knowledge and success.

11.8 The Future of Investing: A Shared Vision

As we look to the future, this chapter reflects on the potential for a shared vision among the community of investors. By aligning on principles of ethical investing, responsible wealth management, and a commitment to positive societal impact, the community can contribute to a future where wealth creation is not only individual but also collective.

Chapter 11 concludes the exploration of Warren Buffett's legacy by highlighting the importance of building a community of investors. Whether through online forums, investment clubs, mentorship, education, or philanthropy, the strength of this community lies in its shared wisdom, collaboration, and commitment to a vision that extends beyond individual wealth.

13

The Evergreen Oracle: Sustaining Buffett's Legacy

Title: "Perpetuating Wisdom: A Blueprint for Future Generations"

12.1 The Continuation of Values: Passing Down Buffett's Principles

Warren Buffett's legacy is not only about financial success but also about the enduring values and principles he embodies. This chapter explores the importance of passing down these principles to future generations. By instilling a commitment to integrity, ethics, and long-term thinking, investors can perpetuate the essence of Buffett's wisdom for years to come.

12.2 The Role of Education: Nurturing the Next Buffett

Education plays a pivotal role in shaping the future of investing. This section emphasizes the importance of educational initiatives that focus on financial literacy, investment principles, and ethical considerations. By nurturing the next generation of investors with a strong educational foundation, we can ensure that the principles espoused by Buffett remain integral to the future of finance.

12.3 Technology and Innovation: Adapting Buffett's Wisdom to Change

As technology and innovation continue to shape the investment landscape, this chapter explores how future investors can adapt Buffett's timeless wisdom to a changing world. By leveraging technology for research, analysis, and collaboration, the next generation can uphold the essence of Buffett's principles while navigating the complexities of an evolving financial ecosystem.

12.4 Sustainability and Social Responsibility: A Cornerstone of Future Investing

The growing emphasis on sustainability and social responsibility is likely to define the future of investing. This section delves into how investors can integrate these considerations into their strategies. By aligning investments with companies that prioritize ESG principles, the next generation can contribute to a more sustainable and ethical financial future.

12.5 Mentorship and Leadership: Guiding Future Stewards of Capital

Mentorship and leadership are critical components of sustaining Buffett's legacy. This chapter emphasizes the role of experienced investors in guiding and shaping the next stewards of capital. Through mentorship programs and leadership initiatives, investors can pass on not just financial acumen but also the ethical and governance principles that underpin Buffett's success.

12.6 Philanthropy as a Driving Force: Impacting Future Generations

Inspired by Buffett's commitment to philanthropy, this section explores the role of future investors in driving positive societal impact. By incorporating philanthropic goals into their wealth management strategies, the next generation can contribute to solving global challenges and leaving a legacy that extends beyond financial success.

12.7 Global Collaboration: Unifying Investors for a Shared Future

The future of investing is likely to be characterized by global collaboration and interconnectedness. This chapter examines how investors can unite across borders, share insights, and collaborate on global challenges. By fostering a sense of shared responsibility and vision, future investors can work together to build a financial landscape that reflects the principles upheld by Buffett.

12.8 A Timeless Blueprint: Building an Evergreen Legacy

As we contemplate the future, this chapter reflects on the timeless blueprint that Warren Buffett's legacy provides. By embracing the principles of integrity, long-term thinking, and ethical investing, future generations can build upon the foundation laid by the Oracle of Omaha. In doing so, they can ensure that Buffett's wisdom remains evergreen, shaping the world of investing for generations to come.

In the concluding chapter, we explore the blueprint for sustaining Warren Buffett's legacy. From passing down values to embracing technology, promoting sustainability, and fostering global collaboration, the future of investing holds immense potential for building upon the principles that have defined Buffett's remarkable journey.

14

Summary

"Oracle of Omaha: Decoding Warren Buffett's Investment Wisdom" takes readers on a comprehensive journey through the life, principles, and legacy of Warren Buffett, one of the most successful investors of all time. The book is structured into twelve chapters, each addressing different facets of Buffett's investment philosophy and its application to contemporary challenges.

Chapter 1 introduces readers to Warren Buffett, outlining his early life, influences, and the core principles that have guided his investment success. Chapters 2 to 8 delve into various aspects of Buffett's investment strategy, exploring his portfolio, principles in action, risk management, ethical foundations, and adaptation to modern markets. Chapter 9 navigates the future of investing, addressing technological advancements, sustainable investing, and other emerging trends.

Chapter 10 serves as a practical guide, offering readers actionable insights into applying Buffett's wisdom to their own investment strategies. Chapter 11 emphasizes the importance of community, discussing investment clubs, mentorship, and the role of philanthropy in creating a supportive network. Finally, Chapter 12 focuses on sustaining Buffett's legacy, passing down values, adapting to change, and building a future of responsible and ethical investing.

Throughout the book, key themes include the importance of knowledge, the circle of competence, patience, quality investing, risk management, ethical considerations, and the enduring impact of Buffett's legacy on the investment community. The narrative encourages readers not only to understand Buffett's principles but also to apply them, adapt to changing landscapes, and contribute to a future of responsible wealth management and positive societal impact.

www.ingramcontent.com/pod-product-compliance
Lightning Source LLC
LaVergne TN
LVHW010438070526
838199LV00066B/6075